G000108280

Songs of a Seeker

Frank Parkinson

OMEGA
POINT PRESS

Published in the United Kingdom in 2017 by

Omega Point Press
14 Ryeheys Road
Lytham St Annes
Lancs. FY8 2HA

Further copies of the book may be obtained from regular booksellers or online from OmegaPointPress.org.uk. where discounted and wholesale terms may be found.

ISBN No. 978-1-901482-01-0

Typeset in Maiandra and Minion Pro by Think Graphics
www.lakeland-webdesign.co.uk

Printed and bound in Great Britain by
TJ International Ltd, Padstow, Cornwall

Contents

Everyday Heaven

Science with Soul

The Journey

Introduction

"Without vision the people perish" (Proverbs 29:18)

It is not usual for writers to explain the meaning of their poems, which are assumed to speak for themselves, but in the present instance there is an overarching theme and a framework which, if made explicit, will add to their meaning and show them all in relationship to each other. Both theme and framework spring from a vision, well expressed in the words of Teilhard de Chardin, "Evolution is a light illuminating all things." A sense of being in the flow of evolution is more even than that: it is a dynamic which urges us on to self-transformation and to transformation of the human species. We cannot understand who we are, nor can I understand who I myself am, until we have looked back into our history to our evolutionary ancestors and back beyond that to our Source – the reality which we conventionally call God - in cosmic time. Nor can we understand ourselves until we have looked forward in imagination to what we can become. There is every reason to think that at some future time the human race can be as far developed from what we are now as we are distant from our ancestors who lived in caves. In this anticipated future human fulfilment will be unambiguously spiritual, as fulfilment in the past was once little more than a successful hunt and a full belly.

If to be more highly evolved implies that we are more spiritually evolved, we need to know more about what "spirituality" means for our time, and in that respect the poems may be taken like dots in a pointillist painting, combining to give an impression, rather than make a formal statement. An impression is, of course, subliminal and cannot be captured in words but, that said, this introduction will make some sort of a try. Speaking oversimply, the poems express a dawning awareness that science and religion as we have known them are passing away and what is to come will be at once a fusion and a transcendence of both modes of knowing. It is only to be expected that the transitional stage will be marked more by confusion than by vision, for the old must first break down before the new can be built. The caterpillar must die before the butterfly can be born.

The greater the new vision the more it will give inspiration and energy, but the more it will be opposed. For not only will it be a step into the unknown, it will threaten all those who have a vested interest in the present. Those whose identity is rooted in the current paradigm and particularly those who exercise authority or gain their living from its structures cannot but resist a genuinely new vision for the future.

The theme that runs as a *leitmov* through the poems is that spirituality itself is evolving and if that be so, a higher kind of spirituality lies ahead and, at the same time, our understanding of what spirituality means must go to a deeper level than in the past. If we are on a spiritual quest, the transformation we both seek and resist must plough deeper. As has been said, the greatest enemy of the best is the good, and this leads us into a paradox that is at the heart of the poems: we both yearn for and resist genuinely new and transforming vision. From that perspective the poems may be taken as a fragmentary account of one person's journey.

Although there remain many details still to be worked out, the new theology opens with "In the beginning was the Big Bang". That is not just a sound bite, but is communicating something with profound significance for both science and religion. Science must decide whether or not the universe is a closed or open system, with something forever beyond our ken, a higher dimensioned reality from which our time-bound, 3-dimensional universe emerged, nearly fourteen billion years ago, when time itself began. At the same time religion must come to terms with the fact that in revealing the processes of cosmic expansion science must be revealing something of importance about the power that brought the universe and each one of us into existence. No longer will there be a problem in harmonising science and religion, for it will be seen that they must be symbiotic, joined at the hip, as the saying goes. Outrageous as this assertion may seem to both scientists and religionists, a genuine religious truth for our time will have to be founded on belief in a creating power that makes sense scientifically. We need a new Isaiah, perhaps a core group of Isaiah's, men and women, to finally sweep away the inadequate understanding of God that is offered by the great faith groups of the world. As the Second Isaiah once railed against the false gods of stone and brass which had "mouths that could not speak, eyes that could not see and ears that could not hear," we need finally to do away with a creating divinity that lives in separation from its creation. We need to live habitually in awareness of the infinite in a grain of sand, a daffodil, the innocence of a child. What now we think of, and dismiss, as mysticism for the rare and gifted few must become a new religious norm, as Karl Rahner, Thomas Berry and other theologians have argued. The "Silence beyond the silence" that is so mysteriously experienced in the mountains or early morning in the garden is very real and far from rare and the challenge to religion today is surely how to develop communication with it, to give ourselves to it. The axial mystery on which most of the poems turn is how this self-giving is returned "in full measure, pressed down and flowing over". No new theology there!

The challenge to science is not so easily summarized, but it will entail acceptance as a fact that consciousness is a form of energy. At a critical period in its evolution science has had to reject this and effectively to deny it, for it had to test out its new method of measurement and experiment on solid, measurable objects. Hence consciousness, or *res cogitans*, had to be excluded from science at the beginning as outside its legitimate subject matter. A shaking of the foundations of science began, however, when physics gained the astounding knowledge that apparently solid matter was actually made of up of energy. A million T-shirts with $E = mc^2$ now pronounce it as common knowledge, but its full significance has yet to emerge. One small fact may serve to indicate what is at issue. To lift a cup of coffee requires a sequence of muscular and electrochemical processes, but all depends on a type of energy which the Nobel laureate Arrhenius called "activational". Nothing happens until I activate the sequence with a conscious decision, which functions as an energetic trigger to set it all in train.

This little fact is food for thought for both theologians and scientists, and the poems may at least offer a few crumbs to whet the appetite. The theology emerging from science supports belief in a creation that is in some sense a manifestation or outflowing of a creating force. The source of the universe and of each individual is in one sense still "out there" but, more importantly, it is immanent within the universe, within nature and within humans more especially. The concept of a divine reality within the material universe and within human consciousness in a special way may at first seem totally unscientific but makes perfect sense if one considers how there can be consciousness encoded "within" a CD before it is expressed acoustically as music or speech. Who or what encoded the consciousness in our DNA is a question that may either be ignored or pondered upon, but those who choose to ignore it have no claim to be better scientists. It is ironic that science should now be presenting the world with a spiritual challenge, but that is the direction in which we are now moving and which all the poems signpost in their different ways.

The agnostic biologist and Nobel laureate Edward O. Wilson has written,

> *Homo sapiens is about to decommission natural selection. Soon we must look deep within ourselves and decide what we wish to become.*

That truly is revelation in the most literal sense, and it faces us all with a complex challenge: do we, as individuals or members of a dedicated community, wish to take part in creating the human-to-be.

It cannot be done from an armchair. It calls for a commitment which was succinctly expressed by Mahatma Gandhi:

> *You yourself must be the change that you wish to see in the world.*

Those two quotations together are the Red Pill that the full vision of evolution holds out for the modern truth-seeker, to be taken or rejected. Like Neo, the Everyman in the cult film *The Matrix*, each of us must make the momentous decision to awaken into a world of reality and unknown challenge or take the Blue Pill and remain in the world of conventional illusion, unchallenged and yet unsatisfied, taking comfort from the crowd or from ritual complaint.

What can be said about the human of future? What kind of creature will *Homo novus* be? The poems assume that the human of the future will be essentially "the new man" which St Paul preached two thousand years ago, but they go beyond Paul's revolutionary vision in important ways, as also beyond the world's other faiths. This surely is to be expected, for we live in a vastly different world to that which was inhabited by Jesus and Paul, Moses, the Buddha, Mohamed, Shankara and the unknown writers of the Vedas. Not only have science and technology changed our normal consciousness but so too have cultural movements such as the Enlightenment, political democracy, gender equality and global communication - to mention only some of the most obvious factors. It would surely be true to say that we are more fully human now than we were then, and that raises the critical question: what prevents us from going forward and unlocking all the potential that at some subliminal level we know we have?

If *Homo novus* is to follow *Homo sapiens*, it will be distinguished by what may be called "noval consciousness". We shall slowly become accustomed to looking out with new eyes into a recentred universe. Against this background the poems may be seen as an attempt to express noval consciousness not only as a recentring of reality but as a change in self-identity, when the full logic of the situation is realised. We are at an evolutionary fork the full significance of which is yet to appear. It will involve a decision as critical as when our distant foreparents came down from the trees, started to walk on two legs and began the long journey from ape to human. What now is involved is a transformation of the ordinary human brain.

The poems, like these thoughts, are fragments of a systematic exposition of that revelation, the realization of which lies in the future. They began, as poems usually do, with isolated flashes of perception and have grown over the years into a small corpus, here organized loosely into five sections, headed *Transformation, Facets of Divinity, Everyday Heaven, Science with Soul and The Journey*. A little explanation of each section may help towards understanding.

Transformation of consciousness is at the heart of human evolution and we can change our consciousness in response to what we desire to be. "Who am I?" and "What am I?" no longer have a single simple answer. Certainly, we are what our genes and our community make us but most importantly we are what we want to be. Neuropsychology has actually shown that we can change our brain physically by creating neural circuits in response to our efforts to attain a goal. Thus spiritual development depends on having as clear a picture as possible of what we want to be. Equally significant, it need hardly be said, is that we must have a reliable method to enable us to achieve it. *Facets of Divinity* contains poems about God, fragments that are as much hopes and questions as theological statements. *Everyday Heaven* is pretty much what the phrase implies, brief encounters with what Hopkins called "the dearest freshness deep down things", when a rose or a sunset or an infant's smile are more than what the ordinary, or even the artistic, eye perceives, when they seem to reach out and grasp us, and perhaps they actually do. *Science with Soul* contains poems that are really a song to science and a thanks for the technology that now enable us to see the most minute and the grandest parts of creation and thus to know more of the Creator and, most importantly, to be aware that we are all now co-creative. That is a radically new theology. *The Journey* celebrates what is too often neglected in our individualistic age, namely, our dependence on the spiritual community for support, encouragement and correction but also a reminder of the responsibility we have for building a spiritual community.

We are all part of the ultimate reality, part of nature and part of each other, and that is in a nutshell what the poems are all about.

Transformation

Declaration of Dependence

Homo Novus

Being and Becoming

Metanoia

The Good Fight

Death Before Birth

Remembrance Day

The Rose and Us

Declaration of Dependence

On that all-important, fateful day
I signed my old self-centred self away
And vowed
That from now on my life would be,
A quest, a task,
To change my nature and identity.

That was the day when I –
That is to say, the new, untested me -
Came blinking from a now discarded chrysalis
And, like the butterfly,
Wobbled a zigzag way into a different sky,
Feeling the power beneath my fragile wings,
Trusting the Source invisible that holds all things.
Little I knew what strength
Would from my voluntary weakness flow,
What certitude from knowing that I did not know.

Homo Novus

What cosmic power, rolling Darwinian dice,
Has taken us from *Homo in-the-raw*,
From hairy Tarzan and his Jane,
Swinging from tree to tree,
Down glacially slow millennia, yet truly
In an evolutionary trice,
To *Homo supremus*, godlets-in-waiting,
Striving to be free,
To breathe a purer air upon a higher plane,
But trapped by man's inherent flaw –
Our forward-seeking, backward-pulling brain.

Our parents in the misty past
Moved on in blind ascent
From Homo testing out two legs -
Erectus-off-and-on -
Stumbling on awkward feet, confused,
But striving all the time to see, to see,
Moving on up to *Homo sapiens* they went,
The wise, wise chimpanzee,
Homo-with-smarts, *Homo-the-proud*,
With sciences and arts so rich endowed,
With music and with poetry,
Mustard gas and cluster bombs
And laser-guided rocketry.

Now here we are, last of our present kind,
At vision's limit, sensing that we now must find
New eyes,
But unsuspecting that this longed for prize
Will make old *Homo* blind.

For round the evolutionary bend
Awaits for our dissecting, restless mind,
At metaphor and logic's end,
A luminescence, cloud without parts
Where we shall find
A marvellous but inside-out new trinity,
An energizing, all-explaining one-in-three:
God beyond religion's god, as Eckhart taught,
An open road to *Homo novus*, so long sought,
And me-beyond-me.

Being and Becoming

What do they know of acorns
Who only acorns know,
Blind to the humdrum miracle
That acorns into oaks will grow.
And what do we know of the form that sleeps
Within our ordinary human shape,
The seed of man-to-be,
The bud that will in its due time unfold,
The story waiting to be told,
The wondrous tale,
The gift of gifts, the Great Escape,
The evolutionary Grail?

Who has the inner eye to see,
Our future and our destiny?
Who has the compass, who the map
On which we now depend?
Where is the friend
To hold our hand and show
The long and winding Way that we must go
To meet our Source and know our End?

Metanoia

Μετανοια (Greek) - Change of Consciousness

Life shapes us with a thousand little strokes,
Sometimes as a sculptor chips and chisels,
Sometimes as a blacksmith hammers
Pounding with unfeeling hands.
Life cuts and saws us like a joiner,
Planes and shaves, abrades and sands.
Wears our patience paper thin,
Rubs right through, reveals to our embarrassment
The unredeemed, half-finished self within.

No pain, no gain; no cross, no crown,
So is the ancient wisdom handed down,
But the Power that gives us power to change
Surely moulds us as a potter
Shapes a formless lump of clay.
And I am moved to think
That if we just accept without complaint
Rough treatment now and then,
God draws out a hidden beauty
From our pear-shaped, lumpy self,
Slowly, surely, day by day,
Silently and tenderly,
In the same unhurried way.

The Good Fight

As Jacob wrestled with an angel,
The messenger of Isra-El -
The struggling God -
I strive to gain transhuman liberty,
To flood my being with the Being
That some fourteen billion years ago
Conceived and bore and nurtured me

Today this grandchild of a Serengeti ape,
Fights the same angel,
But strengthened by the paradox experienced:
Though we must live with surface strife
And the struggle and contention never cease,
God-wrestling brings a richer kind of life
And a deeper sort of peace.

Death before Birth

A second birth occurred,
A different, better me was born.
But future blessing was to come with present cost,
An all-or-nothing trade:
The ego that I once believed was "me"
Fell to the ground, decayed
And, deep inside, the spirit of the past
Released its grip and died.

Then slowly, slowly, cell by cell,
A nobler me took root,
Groped upwards in the trusting dark,
Towards an unknown flowering and fruit,
Seeking the light,
Not knowing then a higher blindness was to be
The longed-for sight.

What vistas open to the human mind
When birth and death are so entwined,
When joy with pain and peace with strife
Fusing create a seventh sense and bring
New energy, new love, new life.

Remembrance Day

Out in the sodden No-man's Land he lay,
His winding sheet
The barbed and tangled, rusting wire,
His monument the blood-soaked clay,

The Unknown Soldier's face stared back at me
Through lifeless eyes
The very emblem of man's ultimate defeat,
Deaf to our patriotic cheers,
Impervious to our too-late tears,
Alone, the alien, the other.

And my heart broke,
As something to my stone dead ears
A word of revelation spoke,
And all at once I knew
You were – you are – my brother.

How could I not have seen the brute insanity
That blinds us to our mother's other child,
That numbs us to this primal sin,
That leads, nay forces, us
To mindless murder of our kith and kin?

Helpless, I look to left and right and ask,
Who now can lead us fratricidal sheep,
What prophet wake us from our deadly sleep?
Who can, with Christlike "Ephphata!",
Open our eyes and hearts?
Oh, will our species never be
Human in kind as well as name,
Truly a global family, that phrase
Which trips so glibly off the tongue
But which we are too hard of heart to feel,
Too dim, too dumb, too tribalised to see?

The Rose and Us

Its peach and scarlet, gold and velvet pink
Reach out and seize our inmost soul,
Its fragrance takes us out of time.
The rose in all its is-ness gives
Ten seconds of infinity,
A foretaste of the Greater Whole,
A warrant of divinity.

But down below the rose we find
A wonder of a different kind.
The rose's sacramental essence springs
From most unspiritual soil –
Though soil's a sacrament as well.
Its roots must share the muck and mire,
With worms and germs and nematodes
And nameless creepy crawly things
Which in that world of darkness dwell.

But, pause,
That lovely rose is not alone,
For if the truth be told –
And beauty only can in truth be found –
We must accept this paradox
In human nature and, closer to the bone,
Right here in me and you.
Our lovely soul, just like our lovely rose,
Has roots in pretty awful ground.
Our would-be higher self we share
With strutting ego and, despite our human shape,
With something not much different from the ape.

But let us not in this uncomfortable state despair.
Take inspiration from the rose's dual life, and know
Our nobler, humbler, patient, generous, loving self
Can only grow
From that dark, ignoble self below.

Facets of Divinity

Mirror, Mirror

God at Prayer

Hootenanny

Romance

Infinity and Me

No Brainer

Goodbye, Monkey Me

Visitation

No Brainer

Praying through Playing

Mirror, Mirror

Razor in hand, I look into the glass
And spy or, rather, half-perceive
The face that looks me in the eye
Seems somehow something more than me.
A deeper soul I see,
My seeking Source, my Ground,
A self renewed, redeemed, refreshed,
Big "R" Reality
In some strange way condensed in me.

Puzzled as by a Necker cube,
Trying to understand this fact sublime.
I see by turns an It, a me, a You,
The mirror's message is a parable,
A sermon for our time,
The ultimate Catch 22.

But if this wild surmise be true,
What does my Source
From Its galactic viewpoint see -
Itself or me?
That childish question turns religion inside out.
Goodbye, the God that lives above and far without,
Welcome, the God without-within.
Hello, Catch 23.

God at Prayer

Speaking as God, I have to say I love you –
Trust me, please!
Breath of my breath, with you I plead.
For heaven's sake (and mine and yours)
Get off your knees.
Lift up your hearts.

Love me for what I am, the Source of love.
Don't listen to those stone age priests
Who think I only dwell above,
Ruling a fallen race with my all-powerful rod.
I wince at all your Lord-have-mercying;
Take it from me, I'm not that sort of God.

Lord knows, I've tried and still I try,
To let you know I'm on your side.
Why can't you see
That all I make is made from me –
The universe entire, the lot:
The space beyond the furthest galaxy,
The silent clarion of the dawn

On Fuji and the Matterhorn,
The lark, the shark, the blossom and the bee,
The duck pond and the wild Atlantic sea.
And you above all,
The apple of my omnipresent eye.
All mine, all me

And all yours too, and more.
Ah, you! - the tender sprig on my great vine,
The drop of homely water in my mystic wine,
The wavelet where my infinite ocean
Meets the shore.
I'm in your deepest heart.
I am your self-of-self within, but you
Must play your part,
For you're a co-creator too.

So please, I pray, I yearn,
Reach up to meet Me as I stoop,
Make it all happen, close the loop,
And give me your little cosmos in return.

Hootenanny: Dancing for God

Age goes, life flows
Stronger than before,
Music's pouring through the window,
Bubbling underneath the door,
Toes are tapping, fingers snapping –
Two, three, four.
Everyone's a-prancing,
A-twirling and a-dancing
On the chairs and on floor,
On the table, on the sideboard,
Stomping on the stairs and landing,
Fit to raise the roof.
Come on, granny, lift your skirts up.
Who needs yoof!

Romance : Dancing with God

We meet at first, just friends,
Learning to know each other's ways,
No grand affair or fine romance,
But then, from time to time we dance.

In closer unison than cheek to cheek,
The It, the Thou and Me are gone.
Act, action, actors, music, movement – all is one.
She feels the pressure of my hand, and gives.
I turn, we turn – has she a seventh sense?
She bends so slightly, as my shoulder falls,
She slows, we pause, her body calls,
And off I go in awe and confidence.

My boldness comes, I am aware,
Not from my skill but hers.
For though she may appear to be
The pliant partner to my Fred Astaire,
Her art my sheer incompetence conceals
And makes a genius of me, a fool.
I gain the freedom that my spirit feels
Because, like Ginger, she inhibits hers.
Thigh, calf and ankle wreathed in tulle,
She moves with infinite skill and flowing grace,
Backwards, but knowing what I see,
And in high heels.

Infinity and Me

Who is the Infinite?
God only knows.
But I am sure
His, Her, Its Spirit flows
And interpenetrates the world,
Seeps, gathers, gushes,
Drives the sweet sap,
Heaves ocean waves and wets the rains.
Spins atom, whirls the galaxies,
Lights the green fuse of nature's bursting life
And pulses in our veins.

All this I daily see and feel.
I touch new worlds,
One with the Cosmic Spirit, yet still two.
Strange paradox, strange silent, plangent mystery!
Who is the Thou and who the me?
I switch my little logic off, and let it be.

No-brainer

The highwayman, twin pistols cocked,
Eyes glaring from his mask,
Yells out, "Your money or your life!"
My cash, snatched with a curse,
Is smartly given up. Some choice!

But God's demand is something worse,
Though made with gentler voice.
"Your money AND your life!"
Not just your bank account and purse
But all you've got,
I want your soul, your life, your very self – the lot.

Don't look so scared, I haven't come to steal.
What looks at first to you like robbery
Is in reality – just take my word –
Jaw-dropping, mind-blowing opportunity,
A once in a hundred life-times deal.

If you hand over all you have – or think you have –
I'll do the same –
Surely the most one-sided swap there ever was.
But just reflect on how I feel:
I'm stuck, even with all the aces in my hand,
I need a partner in this game.

Goodbye, Monkey Me

When will this pestilential ape let go,
When can I finally cast off
This witless, crude impostor me,
Discard the blighter like a grubby coat
And finally set free
The human fully realised I long to be.
No more the timid, spiritual wimp,
Half plaything, half accomplice
Of this chunnering chimp.

Roll on the day
When the really real, the spark of God within,
Takes full control, wins back my soul,
Reanimates my heart,
And gets to grips with life's great work,
To make this half-created self of mine a living part
Within Your Greater Whole.

Visitation

Starlings, avian bandits in the daytime,
Gather for their evening playtime
As from nowhere in an angel crowd,
Sweeping, swooping, swarming, swirling,
Morphing in a living cloud.
Hurling, curling and revolving,
Forming, fading and dissolving,
In celestial display.

Awed by such a visitation,
Dumb, bedazzled, beauty struck,
Comes a reflex from the heart.
I thank the birds and their Creator,
Proof, if any proof were needed,
"That Thou art."

Praying Through Playing

I rejoiced in the inhabited earth, His world,
and my delight was to be
with the children of man. Proverbs 8:31

I play with Wisdom on the shining shore of time,
Cartwheeling with her side by side
Or building towers and parapets of sand
That soon will melt
Like sugar in the next hour's tide.

I play in her Symphonia,
Not with the pros, the famed Celestial Phil,
But in the Band of Hope.
Of hope I sing, with hope I play,
But not much skill.
I watch the baton then the page in fits and starts,
Bluffing my cheerful way through harder parts.
With different instruments I play – to suit my mood
Sometimes a brassy horn I toot,
Sometimes a clarinet or flute,
And when the Spirit gives my fingers wings,
I puff my cheeks and let it go,
And out of sheer exuberance I blow
Wild obligatos on a carefree piccolo.

I play for Paradise United,
Though not the first eleven -
Those in the spiffy shirts of cloth of gold.
As one might guess, there are in heaven
Leagues untold,
And in those ranks of teams beyond infinity
We are the last plus one.
Roy of the Rovers, in my dreams,
Quick as a whippet, tricky, strong and bold,
I whack and nod them in.
And when the game is over
And aetherial mud showered off,
We get together on the club house cloud
To have a post-match drink.
Ambrosia in pints we quaff -
No spirits here in heaven -
And raise a toast,
As glasses of the purest crystal clink:
God bless the game and all that play,
God help God's worst eleven!

Everyday Heaven

Resurrection

The countryside is coming into leaf,
Thrusting, green,
Time-saturated evidence for our belief
In timeless life, eternal energy and love,
Sensed like a hint of fragrance, but not seen,
Life deep within us, all around, above.

After winter's grey and silent cold
The crocuses shine red and gold,
The blackbird and the throstle sing.
Face up, the earth receives warm rain,
The clouds in awesome pageant move,
White on blue,
And wonder falls upon me yet again
At how this mixed-up world of happiness and pain
Dies and returns to life each year on cue
Each reverent, dancing, horn a-blowing
Spring

Special Delivery

For Wendy on the Birth of her Granddaughter

Welcome, bonny bird,
Whose cries we hear,
Whose first brave steps
And first exploring words
Will soon appear.

Welcome, young soul,
Whose every need we seek to know,
To love and give,
Whose growing life will show
Us all, grown-up but all still growing too,
An open-eyed and open-hearted
Way to live.

Was Shakespeare Wrong?

To Richard and Bristi on Their Wedding

When Picu spoke those moving lines,
"Love is not love
Which alters when it alteration finds,"
My heart reached out to you,
But like a richer echo came the thought:
Surely, the opposite is true.
Love *has* to alter when it alteration finds,
For love must deepen, stretch, expand its reach.
Love ripens in the sunshine –
May you have years of sun –
But roots grow stronger in the dark,
When stubborn clouds obscure the dream,
Indeed, when love itself may seem undone.
And that is when it alters,
When the real is really loved,
With all its weaknesses, its quirks and gnarls,
Shadowy corners, holdings back,
Small unsuspected fears.
Virgil said it, *lacrimae rerum* –
No one escapes the tears.
Whatever comes, I have no doubt
Your love will grow and alter, opening out,
Your daily giving, soul to soul
Will recreate each other whole.

Rumi (1207-1273) Through My Prism

Love & Life

Your timeless soul has made its home within
My all-too-present flesh.
Each breath of mine a breath of yours,
Each step, each thought, your life within my life.
Your wish, your will, become a seal
Impressed upon the wax of my surrendering soul.
Your life has changed dead stone to fire.
Your sun by day becomes
Soft moonlight on my night-time heart.

Love in Due Season

I share the glory of your nakedness,
Its welcome, smoother than the finest silk,
Liquid and pure as milk.
Our limbs touch and entwine,
Souls without sin,
Loving in the spring of innocence,
For one sweet moment
Joined in a common destiny
We journey in time
But taste eternity.

Mathnavi

Surrender

In my soul is one small drop of knowing.
Where in Thy ocean can it rest?

Life In Death

Blossom gives way to fruit,
Wheat becomes bread
And bread is broken.
Grapes become wine,
But grapes must be crushed
Before we can taste and drink

Divan

Silence as Salvation

Turn off the word and thought machine,
Let the deepest, silent soul
Start on wordless, all-day prayer,
Bread and butter meditation,
Let God speak through His creation.

Look, look up, survey the skies,
See the clouds that float up there.
Look with newly opened eyes
At the pageant in the air -
Racing skiffs and royal barges,
clipper ships and ghostly galleons
Sailing on a sea serene,
Changing, charming and enchanting,
God's majestic go-between.

Cotton white they float against
Imperial and baby blue,
Performing in celestial liturgy,
Robed in every gorgeous hue,
Orange-silver in the dawn's aurora,
Red-gold backlit at the end of day,
Beautiful in stormy charcoal,
Ravishing in silver grey.
Look in love and in amazement,
Let them pray.

The Rhythm of Life

The corner clock with slow tick-tock
Tells the hours, and this I hear.
The waxing, waning moon records the months,
And this I see.
The hot June sun, the frosted window,
April showers
Mark the seasons as they merge and flow,
And this my senses feel.
But grander still is that great machine,
In a realm unheard, unfelt, unseen,
Where galaxies and planets wheel,
And this with heart and head I know.
I know the maker of this cosmic clock, the Force
That is my deepest self and truest Source,
I touch and taste it with my mind.
This power immense
Reaches my core through every sense
With understanding of a lover's kind.
I seek, am given and sustained
And slowly, imperceptibly, my life entrained,
Made one within the higher life I share.
The daily round, each breath I take,
Each move I make,
Becomes a rhythm and a prayer:
In Your time, at Your speed, for Your sake.

Two Solitudes

Solitude has two faces, I have found.
The first is negative and grey,
The sheer vacuity, the pointlessness,
The trudging round of each dull day,
The loneliness,
Edging sometimes on despair.
Oh yes, I have been there.

But as my higher self has slowly, slowly
Overcome the ego's pull,
What once was emptiness has now become
Richly mysterious and full.

A space once nothing but a void
Within my soul I found
Is occupied by nothing less
Than life itself, my existential ground,
Far from the madding crowd
But filled with the blackbird's carefree song,
The billowing cloud above,
The willow, silver birch and oak,
Faces of children and of old, quite ordinary folk.

Just for Fun

Just for Esther (aged just 8) and Just for Fun

A baker man was kneading dough
And whistling softly, sweet and lough,
But then the flour made him cough,
Fit to make his head come ough,
And he complained,
"My word, this job is rough,
This pesky flour is dreadful stough."
But he kept on,
Punching and pulling through and through,
As expert bakers always dough,
Grumbling, "I'd sooner drive a plough
Than do the job that I have nough."
Thus spoke the baker kneading dough.
This story's true: your dad says sough.

Science with Soul

Quaker Triptych - Time, Space, Infinity

A Cosmologist's Prayer

Co-creation

Creed as Hypothesis

Entrainment

Beyond Science and Religion

Quaker Triptych

Time

Time shapes the hour and prayer shapes time.
The silence holds us like a clear, slow river curling.
Trusting to share this day a touch of the sublime.
Time shapes us like a potter's wheel: the whirling
Energy of God's desire draws up from formless clay
An artifact of love, not stamped but moulded.
Hollowed and smoothed from day to day,
Eternity's design is pass by pass unfolded.
But under the spinning world of God's ambition
The treadling foot performs the vital plod,
The drive and drudge of daily repetition,
Yin of our toil empowering Yang of God.
The flow, the whirl, the plod proceed in phase;
One hour of silent waiting chimes infinities of days.

Space

Elected silence, chooser and chosen one,
Mind's echoes ebbing, peace flows in their place.
The here-now points, extension gone,
Arc and two living realms embrace.
The furnace at the world's primeval heart
Burns out our nature's dross and dirt,
While springs of healing cool the smart
Of love withheld, ambition's fever, all life's hurt.
The Universe entire is in our hand,
And something smaller than a grain of sand –
A self created in annihilation.
Each soul a cell in higher life - a natural wonder!
Within the void we hear God's silent thunder.

Infinity

Passing the bounds of Newton, Cantor, Gauss,
Number dissolves to form a new infinity;
The humblest seeker in the meeting house
Knows, without ciphering, immense divinity.
The light which history in Jesus and his kin reveal
So bright divinity itself shone time-created
Is in this humble room concealed,
Eternal Source in each one incarnated.
And ancient truth that Man is nought
But dust and out of nothing came
Retreats before the sober fact that we are wrought
From God's own stuff, the very same.
Thus one in four evolves from one in three:
Prime lover, Spirit, elder brother - me.

A Cosmologist's Prayer

God of the stars and galaxies,
Herewith a heartfelt *Thank You* for the telescope,
The techno-eye of silicon, titanium and steel,
That gives to our uplifted eyes new hope,
Enables us mole-blind seekers here below
Worlds beyond worlds to view above
And then to feel
Love beyond love.

Gazing without our extra sense,
Poor Pascal, flinching at these *espaces infinies*,
Saw only a freezing void immense, but we,
Gifted with the Hubble and the Webb,
A welcoming hearth beyond can see,
And as our eyes, now super-eyes, the cosmos roam,
Your universe becomes our natural home,
And what at first appear as realms apart begin
To work upon and infiltrate our mind and heart:
Your world without becomes our world within,
And distant music of the spheres,
Amplified by new-tuned ears,
Swells in a great *Te Deum*.

Thus cosmo-science shapes our minds and hearts
To know and feel
That the same all-mighty force
Which holds the heavenly bodies in their course
Draws us all back to you, our source,
And with Augustine we are moved to say
Amor meus pondus meum –
Love is our gravity.

Co-creation

Once, like everyone, I asked
What was the Grand Design,
The unimaginable Will
That lit the primordial fuse
Which blew to life
A wondrous realm of galaxies,
Starting with a Planckian dot of energy
And expanding still.

But where was the Source of this amazing Plan?
Where was the Deity before it all began?
What came before this hyperspatial Force
To give new meaning to our vacuous word
"infinity"?
What, if logic holds, must be
Of all created things the Primal Source,
The Ultimate Divinity?

The dizzying regress of a
God-creating-God-creating-God,
Numbs logic, turns it on itself, and yet
A simpler logic rules.

I see, and feel
The truth that purblind atheists have missed,
This known-unknown Reality must have been
In at the unfathomable start,
Since I am here and now.
No longer *Cogito et ergo sum*
But *Sum et ergo ist*.

The greater wonder now I see,
Is that in a less than humble fragment
Of its three-dimensioned, time-bound form
This Power has made its home and seeds its very Self
Within my soul, from which it follows, unbelievably,
Terrestrial creation now has need of me,
A small but useful part.

So then what sort of hybrid entities are we,
Creature and creator all in one?
The Grand Design has truly just begun.

Creed as Hypothesis

Everything within our world
And all the worlds that coexist
Is but a showing forth
Of the Great Reality that is our Source,
The power that we call God.

From its primordial Energy
We are spun,
From Its Life we take our life.
We are because It is.

Our time-dimensioned self was there
Within the universe's seed,
Within the point of densest Light
When time and space began.

By this Eternal Energy we are loved,
With It we can communicate,
And in communicating
Share its Being.

This paradox rules all:
The Life that gave us life,
This Infinite Power, is in our power,
Its time-bound future in our hands.

Its hopes our prayers,
Its purposes with ours entwined,
Its consciousness reflected
In the mirror of our mind.

Entrainment

Now here's the thing, the secret balm,
The power to smooth away
The stress and strife of each frenetic,
Go-round, not so merry day,
To slow things down, to regulate, to heal, to calm.
The answer is quite simple

We must be still and start again,
Recalibrate our oh-so-busy,
So important little lives and harmonize
Them with a Higher Will,
Know each moment in its flight
For what it really is,
A golden fragment in an unseen plan
Unfolding out of sight,
Guided by an unseen Mind.

So will we find
That ever closer to this rhythm bound,
And imperceptibly uniting, ground to Ground,
Each day its unexpected blessing brings,
Learning to really be, to really know,
Sharing the energy that wound the universe's
    springs,
Roaming where only angels are supposed to go.

Beyond Science and Religion

Where there is no longer time
or place,
No longer word
or even thought,
There in the silence
and the waiting,
There in the darkness,
in the longing and confusion
Seeps our true knowing –
Honey from the rock.

The Journey

Heaven or Bust

Magic Mountain

The Wind Beneath Our Wings

Pulling Together

Theotrope

Soul Food

Chickology

A Song to True Religion

Heaven or Bust

It's a strange old trail, up hill, down dale,
In the search for self and the quest for God.
When it's sunny and bright and all feels right,
I can hum a little song, as I swing along,
But it's more of a shuffle and a silent plod
When the sun disappears
And lurking in the hedge are whispering fears
That I might after all be wrong.

For it's easy to forget, when black clouds swell
And the mists of doubt surround,
That the Source we seek seeks us as well,
And won't give up till It has found
Our holographic self to share its Soul
For our ultimate Source must too be whole.

Magic Mountain

Onward and upward, keep on with the climb,
Sooner or later my Maker I'll meet,
All in good time -
So I thought.

But our meeting was not of the usual sort.
No trumpets, no bells, no "Eureka!", no "Wow!"
For just as I'm starting to feel I am winning,
I find myself at a new sort of beginning.
What to do now?

The view from the top is not what I had dreamed,
Success in the quest is not what it had seemed,
For the peak, I now find, is the edge of a cliff,
And the end of my climb is a daunting "What if?"

What if I keep on and step into the void,
Will I lose the whole game or find Truth unalloyed?
I pause to take stock, but the feeling "I must"
Swells to a challenge I cannot evade.
In one scary moment the choice is made:
Eyes open, deep breath, step forward
And trust.

The Wind Beneath Our Wings

Playing the thermals, high in a cloudless sky
The circling eagle rides,
Silently preaching the mystery,
Of Thou-and-I,
For as it effortlessly glides,
Its motion brings
A message to us here below of higher, purer things.
Watching that bird aloft reveals -
Nay, generates –
The sense of power that surely in its flight it feels.
Transfixed, my heart more deeply knows
The force that holds the bird,
The world entire and us, the great reality,
The wind beneath our wings.

Pulling Together

Straining with frosted breath they go.
Mush! Mush! Away they go,
The gang line and the tug line tense,
Sled tracks lengthen in the sparkling snow

The master's voice
Is answered by the yelping choir.
On his command they run
Constrained but freely, eagerly, by choice,
Pulling together side by side,
Taking their rhythm and their stride
From the servant-leader dog,
All know their worth,
All know their part.

Can anything on earth
So warm the human heart
As the joy of running, bound but free,
Like huskies in their work,
Led by a voice we hear but cannot see,
Impelled towards a place we do not know,
Feeling only the desire to be.

Theotrope

Hopkins said that dragonflies catch flame,
And every mortal thing
Behaves the same,
Showing – to those who have an inward eye -
A flash, a radiance within.

And we, half God, half naked chimpanzee,
What inner fire do we display?
What glow within do other people see?
What canst thou say?

Say nothing now, stand still.
Stay mute until
Loving awareness starts to turn
Towards the eternal sun.
Let go, let God,
Go to the heliotrope to learn.

Soul Food

The world around is full of grace.
Daily like the Hebrews in the desert
We are fed,
Not with manna from above
Nor with ordinary bread
But with an oft unnoticed touch of love.
With sun and wind upon our face,
Cold of frost and warmth of fire,
Dawn and dusk in golden red,
Music from a garden choir.

Each quite natural sensation,
Once reflected in our mind,
Becomes a moment of creation,
Nourishes and makes us whole,
Awakes our spiritual appetite
And satisfies the soul.

Chickology

Peck, peck, keep pecking through the ego-shell.
Break from the warm, dark world of ignorance,
The Matrix where we unsuspecting dwell.
Become a creature of the light,
A being of a higher kind.
Peck through to find the brave, new world
That beckons to your inmost soul
And you will find
That what you fear may blind
Your feeble, never tested eyes
Will in reality endow you with
A different, more revealing sight,
And in due course will bind you in
A global family of the wise.

A Song to True Religion

We ought to seek a confraternity
Bound together in belief
That true religion is a quest
For unity of self with God
And self with other selves.

A true community should be
The daily actions that we share,
The round of work and play, of table time,
Of song and prayer,

A true religion coaxes all to grow,
To see what old religion never saw,
With mind and heart to know
That we are of the Infinite a finite part
And understand that three-word mystery,
That Thou art,
At once a love song and a law.

Other books by Frank Parkinson

Science and Religion at the Crossroads

The Global Energy Trap and a Way Out

Religion without Fairy Tales

God Evolving (2018)